W9-APC-393

Let's Learn Katakana

Second Book of Basic Japanese Writing

Yasuko Kosaka Mitamura

Let's Learn Katakana

Let's Learn Katakana

Yasuko Kosaka Mitamura

KODANSHA INTERNATIONAL
Tokyo・New York・London

Distributed in the United States by Kodansha America, LLC, and in the
United Kingdom and continental Europe by Kodansha Europe Ltd.

Published by Kodansha International Ltd., 17–14 Otowa 1-chome,
Bunkyo-ku, Tokyo 112–8652.

Copyright © 1985 by Yasuko Kosaka Mitamura.
All rights reserved. Printed in Japan.
ISBN 978–0–87011–719–0
ISBN 978–4–7700–1219–7 (in Japan)
LCC 85–40059

First edition, 1985
20 19 18 17 16 15 14 13 12 11 10   30 29 28 27 26 25 24 23

www.kodansha-intl.com

Contents

PREFACE

Up until now, the significance of Katakana in written Japanese has been neglected in teaching Japanese as a foreign language. Even students who become familiar with the symbols often do not have a clear understanding of the entire Katakana syllabary and its many applications.

For the most part, the conventional method of introducing Katakana in Japanese language instruction has been limited to words of foreign origin. A shortcoming of this method is that it emphasized reading Katakana and did not provide sufficient practice in writing. In fact, only basic everyday words such as those for chocolate, handkerchief, ice cream, milk, necktie and the like were used as examples.

Actually, Katakana is not confined to foreign words; the ways it is used are extremely varied, and it is often the appropriate way to write many Japanese words, such as the names of plants and animals, onomatopoeic expressions, domestic telegrams and so on. The most conspicuous use of Katakana is seen in the recent trend to give words a special nuance, usually by stressing certain words to make them stand out. This new use is found in all the latest magazines and advertisements and seems to be on the increase.

Due to the varied and expanding use of Katakana, teaching needs to be updated. Students should be able to read and write Katakana, as well as know when to use it. Continual practice and exposure to Katakana, as provided by diligent use of this workbook, will lead to eventual mastery of this form of writing.

This workbook has been designed, like its companion volume *Let's Learn Hiragana*, with sufficient explanation and examples to allow students of Japanese to learn Katakana on their own, without the aid of an instructor. Special note should be made of the fact that the words in the examples and exercises are not words ordinarily written in Hiragana and here transcribed into Katakana for the sake of instruction. They are words carefully selected because they are always or in certain circumstances written in Katakana.

There are five chapters in this book. Chapter 1 introduces the forty-six basic Katakana and twenty-three modified symbols. The contracted syllables, and the twenty-five additional syllables found only in Katakana, are given in chapter 2, which first explains the general guidelines for writing words in Katakana. Chapter 3 shows various words of Japanese origin that are written in Katakana. Chapter 4 gives guidelines and exercises for transcribing foreign words into Katakana. In chapter 5 there are review exercises. Answers to the exercises are given in Appendix A, and the derivation of Katakana is outlined in Appendix B.

For convenience, the format of this workbook has been kept the same as the companion Hiragana book. As in the previous volume, the Modified Hepburn System is used throughout for Romanization of Japanese words.

I would like to give special thanks to Mr. Minoru Yasunaga, senior specialist, Japanese Language Division of the Ministry of Education, for taking precious time to provide me with much invaluable information.

I would also like to thank the following people for their contributions to this workbook: my dear friend Virginia Newton, for editing various drafts of the manuscript; my niece Akiko Kosaka, who helped in the time-consuming process of selecting the vocabulary for the examples and exercises; and my daughter Joyce, for her assistance in every phase of the work from the first to the final draft.

1

HOW TO WRITE SYLLABLES

As you know, there are two types of writing in Japanese: Kanji and Kana. Kanji are Chinese ideographs which have been used in Japan for about fifteen hundred years, whereas Kana are phonetic symbols representing pronunciation. There are two Kana syllabaries: Hiragana and Katakana. Both of them are derived from Kanji.

Hiragana and Katakana developed almost simultaneously, but independently and for different reasons. This took place a little over a thousand years ago. (A note on the history of Katakana is given in Appendix B.)

To better understand the relationship between the three ways of writing Japanese, one might think of Hiragana as being a sort of guide wheel, for it underlies the writing system as a whole. Kanji, on the other hand, has played an important role historically in expressing the many words and concepts whose original source is the Chinese language. In modern usage, Katakana bears the burden of representing words whose origins are foreign languages other than Chinese. All three are indispensable to read and write Japanese.

As noted, the relationship between Kanji and vocabulary of Chinese origin is very close, so in the present context *foreign words* refers to words from other languages. The majority of these vocabulary items are words from Western languages, especially English. (It is not unknown for Chinese words to be written in Katakana, but the total number is quite small.)

Words borrowed from "other" foreign languages are customarily felt to belong to one of two categories: loanwords (*gairaigo*) or, simply, foreign words (*gaikokugo*). Words in the first group, either because of the frequency with which they are used or the length of time since they began to be used, have been assimilated. These foreign words are used for a variety of reasons, ranging from the need for precise definition, as in scientific work, through an interest in preserving the particular nuance or affect a word can have, to an urge to be "with it," as with items of pop culture. Of course, in certain cases it is not easy, even for the specialist, to say whether a particular word has or has not been fully assimilated.

Because Katakana symbols are not a cursive style like Hiragana, they have sharp angles, more straight lines and fewer curves, making them perhaps a little easier to master. However, in terms of basic communication, Hiragana is by far the more frequently encountered and should be learned first.

One point which Hiragana and Katakana have in common is that in both systems one Kana represents one syllable. And there are five types of syllables in Katakana, just as there are in Hiragana:

1. Five basic vowels: [a], [i], [u], [e], [o]
2. Consonant or semivowel + vowel: [na], [ki], [yu], etc.
3. Syllabic consonant: [n]/[m]
4. Any consonant other than [n]/[m] when followed by another identical consonant, e.g., *koppu*, *yotto*, etc.
5. A contracted syllable: [ki] + [ya] = [kya], [chi] + [ya] = [cha], etc.

In preparation for the introduction of the Katakana symbols, it is important to first mention the general rules for writing them. These rules are exactly the same in Katakana as in Hiragana. Stroke order must be memorized for each symbol. The general rule for stroke order is left to right ⟶ and top to bottom ↓ . Ending a stroke correctly is equally important. As you will remember, there are three different ways to do this: *tome*, *hane* and *harai*. Tome means "stop," so you bring the pen or pencil to a complete stop and lift it off the paper. The tome ending is indicated by a dot placed at the end of the stroke in the following examples:

エ   キ   ト

The second ending, hane, means "jump." Therefore you end the stroke by abruptly lifting the pen or pencil off the paper. This is indicated by a check mark ∨ in the following examples:

The final ending, harai, means "sweep." You execute this by lifting the pen or pencil up gradually at the end of the stroke while your hand is still in motion. This is indicated by a dotted line in the following examples:

On pages 12 and 13 is the complete Katakana syllabary. It is presented in two parts. In table I, the first section contains the forty-six basic symbols. The second and third sections contain the three forms of modification, *dakuon* (indicating voicing of consonant), *handakuon* (for semivoicing) and *yōon* (contracted syllables). Up to this point the Katakana syllabary is quite the same as the Hiragana syllabary. Both the pronunciation and the *rōmaji* are exactly the same. In table II, you will find the expanded syllabary consisting of twenty-five additional syllables used only when writing foreign words.

The reason for the expanded syllabary is to signal the pronunciation of sounds that are not found in Japanese. In *Let's Learn Hiragana*, we observed that about thirty-eight sounds are necessary to speak English. If English and Japanese are compared, it will be seen that the number of sounds required for Japanese is approximately ten to twelve less than the minimum necessary for English. Hence, the existence of the expanded syllabary to account for pronunciation that occurs in English—or other languages—but not in Japanese.

After familiarizing yourself with both parts of the syllabary, turn to page 14, where you can begin learning the basic Katakana, one group at a time, by studying the text and doing the exercises. Each successive group of exercises includes Katakana from previous exercises.

TABLE I: BASIC KATAKANA SYLLABARY

1. 46 Basic Katakana

	a	ka	sa	ta	na	ha	ma	ya	ra	wa	n/m
	ア	カ	サ	タ	ナ	ハ	マ	ヤ	ラ	ワ	ン
	イ (i)	キ (ki)	シ (shi)	チ (chi)	ニ (ni)	ヒ (hi)	ミ (mi)		リ (ri)		
	ウ (u)	ク (ku)	ス (su)	ツ (tsu)	ヌ (nu)	フ (fu)	ム (mu)	ユ (yu)	ル (ru)		
	エ (e)	ケ (ke)	セ (se)	テ (te)	ネ (ne)	ヘ (he)	メ (me)		レ (re)		
	オ (o)	コ (ko)	ソ (so)	ト (to)	ノ (no)	ホ (ho)	モ (mo)	ヨ (yo)	ロ (ro)	ヲ (o)	

2. 18 Dakuon and 5 Handakuon

	ga	za	da	ba	pa
	ガ	ザ	ダ	バ	パ
	ギ (gi)	ジ (ji)		ビ (bi)	ピ (pi)
	グ (gu)	ズ (zu)		ブ (bu)	プ (pu)
	ゲ (ge)	ゼ (ze)	デ (de)	ベ (be)	ペ (pe)
	ゴ (go)	ゾ (zo)	ド (do)	ボ (bo)	ポ (po)

3. 33 Yōon

21 Basic Yōon

	kya	sha	cha	nya	hya	mya	rya
	キャ	シャ	チャ	ニャ	ヒャ	ミャ	リャ
	キュ (kyu)	シュ (shu)	チュ (chu)	ニュ (nyu)	ヒュ (hyu)	ミュ (myu)	リュ (ryu)
	キョ (kyo)	ショ (sho)	チョ (cho)	ニョ (nyo)	ヒョ (hyo)	ミョ (myo)	リョ (ryo)

9 Dakuon / 3 Handakuon

	gya	ja	bya	pya
	ギャ	ジャ	ビャ	ピャ
	ギュ (gyu)	ジュ (ju)	ビュ (byu)	ピュ (pyu)
	ギョ (gyo)	ジョ (jo)	ビョ (byo)	ピョ (pyo)

TABLE II: ADDITIONAL SYLLABLES FOR FOREIGN WORDS

16 Additional Syllables

fa ファ		*tsa* ツァ	*cha*	*sha*	*kwa* クァ	*kya*		
fi フィ	*ti* ティ						*wi* ヴィ	
fu			*chu*	*shu*		*kyu*		
fe フェ		*tse* ツェ	*che* チェ	*she* シェ			*we* ウェ	*ye* イェ
fo フォ		*tso* ツォ	*cho*	*sho*	*kwo* クォ	*kyo*	*wo* ヲ	

9 Additional Syllables

va ヴァ		*ja*	*gwa* グァ	*gya*
vi ヴィ	*di* ディ			
vu ヴ	*dyu* デュ	*ju*		
ve ヴェ		*je* ジェ		
vo ヴォ		*jo*		

a	ア		
i	イ		
u	ウ		
e	エ		
o	オ		
ka	カ		
ki	キ		
ku	ク		
ke	ケ		
ko	コ		
sa	サ		
shi	シ		
su	ス		
se	セ		
so	ソ		

a	ア	ア	
i	イ	イ	
u	ウ	ウ	
e	エ	エ	
o	オ	オ	
ka	カ	カ	
ki	キ	キ	
ku	ク	ク	
ke	ケ	ケ	
ko	コ	コ	
sa	サ	サ	
shi	シ	シ	
su	ス	ス	
se	セ	セ	
so	ソ	ソ	

First Group

As shown on the previous pages, the first group of fifteen basic Katakana consists of the five basic vowels [a], [i], [u], [e], [o] and the ten syllables combining *k* or *s/sh* with these vowels.

These fifteen Katakana have ten dakuon: [ga], [gi], [gu], [ge], [go] and [za], [ji], [zu], [ze], [zo]. The symbolic representation of the voicing of the consonants in Katakana is the same as in Hiragana: two abbreviated strokes are added at the upper right corner of the symbol. For example, [ka] is 力 and [ga] is 力゛; [ki] is キ and [gi] is ギ and so on.

Exercises

A. Fill in each space with the appropriate Katakana to make words.

1. ___ イ ス (ice)
   a

2. ___ 力 (squid)
   i

3. ___ サ ギ (rabbit)
   u

4. ___ ア (air)
   e

5. ___ ア シ ス (oasis)
   o

6. ス イ ___ (watermelon)
   ka

7. ___ ス (kiss)
   ki

9. サ ___ (salmon)
   ke

10. ___ ___ ア (cocoa)
    ko *ko*

11. ___ ギ (heron)
    sa

12. ___ 力 (deer)
    shi

13. 力゛ ___ (gas)
    su

14. ___ コ イ ア (sequoia)
    se

15. シ ___ (shiso)
    so

16

8. キ <u>　　</u> (chrysanthemum)
　　　<small>ku</small>

B. Write the following words in Katakana.

    1. *iesu* (yes)　　　　　　5. *kuizu* (quiz)　　　　　9. *aji* (horse mackerel)

    2. *ushi* (cow)　　　　　　6. *koke* (moss)　　　　　10. *sekaseka* (restless)

    3. *ka* (mosquito)　　　　　7. *koi* (carp)　　　　　11. *Ajia* (Asia)

    4. *kishikishi* (squeak)　　　8. *saizu* (size)　　　　12. *ekisu* (extract)

C. Read the following words and write them in Romanized Japanese.

    1. アシカ (sea lion)　　　　　6. クスクス (giggle)

    2. ウグイス (nightingale)　　　7. ケシ (poppy)

    3. スエズ (Suez)　　　　　　8. アサガオ (morning glory)

    4. アカシア (acacia)　　　　　9. カサカサ (rustle)

    5. スギ (Japanese cedar)　　　10. スコア (score)

ta	タ			
chi	チ			
tsu	ツ			
te	テ			
to	ト			
na	ナ			
ni	ニ			
nu	ヌ			
ne	ネ			
no	ノ			
ha	ハ			
hi	ヒ			
fu	フ			
he	ヘ			
ho	ホ			

ta	タ	タ
chi	チ	チ
tsu	ツ	ツ
te	テ	テ
to	ト	ト
na	ナ	ナ
ni	ニ	ニ
nu	ヌ	ヌ
ne	ネ	ネ
no	ノ	ノ
ha	ハ	ハ
hi	ヒ	ヒ
fu	フ	フ
he	ヘ	ヘ
ho	ホ	ホ

Second Group

The second group consists of the three subgroups made by combining *t/ch/ts* or *n* or *h/f* with the basic vowels to form the syllables [ta], [chi], [tsu], [te], [to]; [na], [ni], [nu], [ne], [no]; and [ha], [hi], [fu], [he], [ho].

Along with the above fifteen basic Katakana, there are three dakuon counterparts of [ta], [te], [to]; these are [da], [de], [do]. The [ha], [hi], [fu], [he], [ho] subgroup also has the two sets of modification: [ba], [bi], [bu], [be], [bo]; and [pa], [pi], [pu], [pe], [po].

It is important to note that the voiced counterparts of シ [shi] and チ [chi], which are ジ [ji] and ヂ [ji], are pronounced the same, as are the voiced counterparts of ス [su] and ツ [tsu], which have the same pronunciation [zu] and are written ズ and ヅ respectively. However, in Katakana, unlike in Hiragana, ヂ [ji] and ヅ [zu] are no longer needed or used, and therefore do not appear in the syllabary.

Exercises

D. Fill in each space with the appropriate Katakana to make words.

1. ___ イ (sea bream)
　　ta

2. ___ クタク (ticktock)
　　chi

3. バケ ___ (bucket)
　　　　tsu

4. ___ ス ___ (test)
　　te　　*to*

5. ___ イフ (knife)
　　na

6. テ ___ ス (tennis)
　　　ni

8. ___ クタイ (necktie)
　　ne

9. ピ°ア ___ (piano)
　　　　no

10. ___ イ (pie)
　　pa

11. エ ___ (shrimp)
　　　bi

12. ___ ナ (Crucian carp)
　　fu

13. ___ ビ (snake)
　　he

20

7. アイ ___ (Ainu)
   nu

14. ___ ス (boss)
    bo

E. Write the following words in Katakana.

1. *itachi* (weasel)

2. *tsutsuji* (azalea)

3. *kani* (crab)

4. *tanuki* (raccoon dog)

5. *kitsune* (fox)

6. *inoshishi* (boar)

7. *basu* (bus)

8. *hinoki* (cypress)

9. *fuji* (wisteria)

10. *hechima* (snake gourd)

11. *hosutesu* (hostess)

12. *paionia* (pioneer)

F. Read the following words and write them in Romanized Japanese.

1. カクタス (cactus)

2. ツバキ (camellia)

3. テキサス (Texas)

4. ドア (door)

5. ウナギ (eel)

6. ニコニコ (smilingly)

7. イヌ (dog)

8. ネコ (cat)

9. イセエビ (lobster)

10. ヘトヘト (exhausted)

ma	マ	⇗ヲ	マ
mi	ミ	ミ	ニ	ミ
mu	ム	∠	ム
me	メ	ノ	メ
mo	モ	ニ	ニ	モ
ya	ヤ	⇗ヲ	ヤ
yu	ユ	⇗ユ	ユ
yo	ヨ	ヲ	ヲ	ヨ
ra	ラ	ニ	ラ
ri	リ	↓!	リ
ru	ル	⌐	ル
re	レ	↙レ	レ
ro	ロ	↓!	ロ	ロ
wa	ワ	↓!	ワ
o	ヲ	ニ	ニ	ヲ
n/m	ン	ン	ン

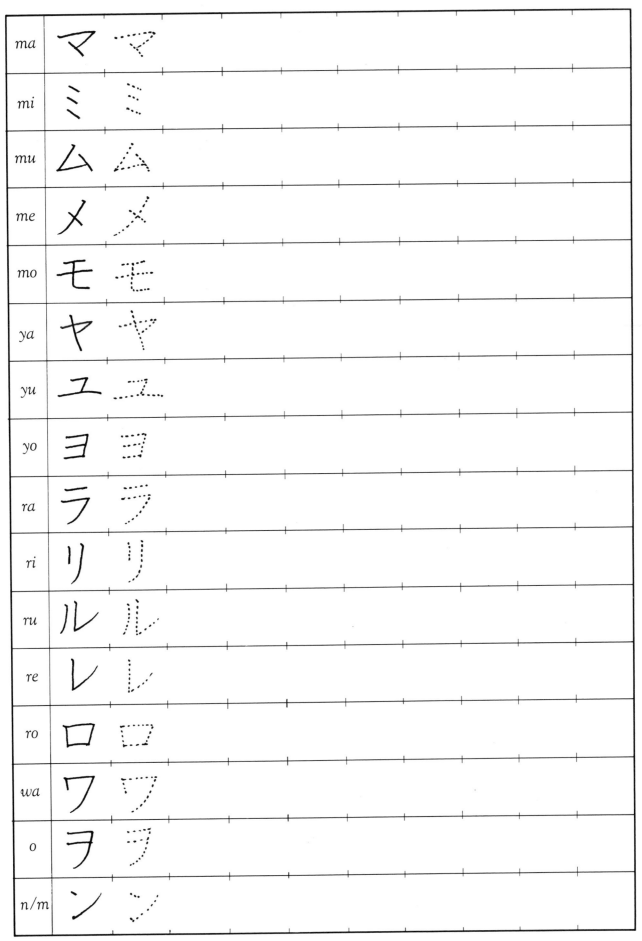

ma	マ
mi	ミ
mu	ム
me	メ
mo	モ
ya	ヤ
yu	ユ
yo	ヨ
ra	ラ
ri	リ
ru	ル
re	レ
ro	ロ
wa	ワ
o	ヲ
n/m	ン

Third Group

In the third group of sixteen basic Katakana, the first five combine *m* with the vowels to form [ma], [mi], [mu], [me], [mo]. The next three combine *y* with three of the basic vowels to form [ya], [yu] and [yo]. The next five Katakana combine *r* with the vowels to give [ra], [ri], [ru], [re], [ro].

The next symbol, [wa], represents the semivowel [w] + [a]. Just as in Hiragana, the syllables [wi], [wu] and [we] do not exist in the basic Katakana syllabary. (However, [wi], [we] and [wo] are among the additional syllables in the expanded syllabary.)

In Hiragana, as you know, the syllable in this column represented by the symbol を [o], has an important grammatical function. The fifteenth symbol in this group ヲ [o] also exists, but it is rarely encountered. Generally speaking, particles are omitted in domestic telegrams. However, if it were necessary to specify the particle *o* for the sake of clarity, this is the symbol that would be employed. ヲ might also be found in historical documents.

The final symbol in this group represents the syllable [n]/[m]. Remember, this is a syllable in itself and it differs from the syllables formed by *n* or *m* plus a vowel.

Exercises

G. Fill in each space with the appropriate Katakana to make words.

1. ト ___ ト (tomato)
   ma

2. ___ ルク (milk)
   mi

3. ハ ___ (ham)
   mu

4. カ ___ ラ (camera)
   me

9. ク ___ ス (class)
   ra

10. ___ スト (list)
    ri

11. タオ ___ (towel)
    ru

12. テ ___ ビ゛ (television)
    re

24

5. メ ___ (memo)
      mo

6. タイ ___ (tire)
        ya

7. ___ リ (lily)
   yu

8. ___ セミテ (Yosemite)
   yo

13. ___ シア (Russia)
    ro

14. ___ シ (eagle)
    wa

15. レモ ___ (lemon)
        n

16. レ ___ ズ (lens)
       n

H. Write the following words in Katakana.
1. *omuretsu* (omelet)

2. *kumo* (spider)

3. *yagi* (goat)

4. *yunion* (union)

5. *raten* (Latin)

6. *mainasu* (minus)

7. *mineraru* (mineral)

8. *romansu* (romance)

9. *waifu* (wife)

10. *hankachi* (handkerchief)

I. Read the following words and write them in Romanized Japanese.

1. マラソン (marathon)

2. スタミナ (stamina)

3. アルバム (album)

4. ユネスコ (UNESCO)

7. レイ (lei)

8. リス (squirrel)

9. プログラム (program)

10. ズボン * (trousers)

5. モナコ (Monaco)　　　11. ミラクル (miracle)

6. アヤメ (iris)　　　12. クリスマス (Christmas)

*From French, *jubon*

2

HOW TO WRITE WORDS

Now you have learned the forty-six basic Katakana and their dakuon and han-dakuon. The next symbols shown in the syllabary are the yōon. Before learning how to use contracted syllables in making words, it is important to know some symbols and the general rules for writing words in Katakana.

[o]+[o] in Japanese Words

As you may recall, in Hiragana the writing of double o's (oo, ō) received special attention. When double o's occur, the second [o] was in most cases written as う [u], and only in a few cases as お [o]. This same rule applies in Katakana writing, but only for words of Japanese origin. (Other cases are taken up in the next section of this chapter.) When ō occurs, the second [o] is most often written with ウ [u]. There are some exceptions using オ [o].

ウ [u] for the second [o]:

bu	do	o (grape)
ブ	ド	ウ

sa	ku	ra	m	bo	o (cherry)
サ	ク	ラ	ン	ボ	ウ

ho	o	re	n	so	o (spinach)
ホ	ウ	レ	ン	ソ	ウ

go	bo	o (burdock)
ゴ	ボ	ウ

sa	to	o	ki	bi (sugar cane)
サ	ト	ウ	キ	ビ

to	o	mo	ro	ko	shi (corn)
ト	ウ	モ	ロ	コ	シ

zo	o (elephant)
ゾ	ウ

o	o	mu (parrot)
オ	ウ	ム

ko	o	mo	ri (bat)
コ	ウ	モ	リ

ko	o	no	to	ri (stork)
コ	ウ	ノ	ト	リ

オ [o] for the second [o]:

ho	*o*	*ji*	*ro* (meadow bunting)		*o*	*o*	*mu*	*gi* (barley)
ホ	オ	ジ	ロ		オ	オ	ム	ギ

o	*o*	*ka*	*mi* (wolf)		*ho*	*o*	*zu*	*ki* (ground-cherry)
オ	オ	カ	ミ		ホ	オ	ズ	キ

Other Double Vowels

In writing foreign words in Katakana, when any vowel is lengthened a short straight line is used instead of writing the symbol for that vowel. This long-vowel mark occupies the same space as one Katakana symbol: — for horizontal writing, ｜ for vertical writing. The same rule applies, too, when writing onomatopoeia. Examples of this are given in chapter 3.

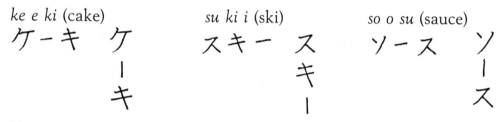

ke e ki (cake) 　　　*su ki i* (ski) 　　　*so o su* (sauce)

Exercises

A. Write the following words in katakana, using — for the long vowel.

1. *aisukurīmu* (ice cream)　　　6. *gēmu* (game)

2. *kādo* (card)　　　7. *chīzu* (cheese)

3. *kōto* (coat)　　　8. *nōto* (notebook)

4. *kōhī* (coffee)　　　9. *bīru* (beer)

5. *sūpu* (soup)　　　10. *bōto* (boat)

B. Write the following words in Katakana, paying special attention to the long vowel.

1. *apāto* (apartment)

2. *erebētā* (elevator)

3. *kī* (key)

4. *shītsu* (sheet)

5. *sōsēji* (sausage)

6. *tākī* (turkey)

7. *tēburu* (table)

8. *bōru* (ball)

9. *mētoru* (meter)

10. *rēsu* (race)

C. Read the following words and write them in Romanized Japanese.

1. エネルギー * (energy)

2. カレーライス (curried rice)

3. コーラス (chorus)

4. シーズン (season)

5. スプーン (spoon)

6. スケート (skate)

7. デパート (department store)

8. ハーモニカ (harmonica)

9. ベースボール (baseball)

10. レコード (record)

*From German, *Energie*

The method of writing double consonants in Katakana is exactly the same as in Hiragana. With the exception of [n]/[m], the first of any pair of double consonants is always written with a half-size ツ (*tsu*). Look at the following examples.

ma t chi (match)
マッチ

ko p pu (cup)
コップ°

As explained in *Let's Learn Hiragana*, the half size ツ is not pronounced but indicates a time beat of one syllable in duration.

What looks like double [n] or [m] in rōmaji does not follow the example above. As in Hiragana, the first [n] or [m] is the syllabic [n]/[m], and the second [n] or [m] belongs to the following syllable, as in these examples.

to n ne ru (tunnel)
ト ン ネ ル

ma m mo su (mammoth)
マ ン モ ス

Exercises

D. Write the following words in Katakana, paying special attention to the underlined consonant.

1. ku <u>k</u> kī (cookie)

2. ra ke <u>t</u> to (racquet)

3. sa <u>k</u> kā (soccer)

4. so <u>k</u> ku su (socks)

5. to ra <u>k</u> ku (truck)

6. na <u>t</u> tsu (nut)

7. no <u>k</u> ku (knock)

8. pe <u>t</u> to (pet)

E. First count the number of syllables, then write the following words in Katakana.

1. appuru (apple)

6. netto (net)

30

2. *kurejitto* (credit)   7. *battā* (batter)

3. *kokku** (cook)   8. *hitto* (hit)

4. *sukippu* (skip)   9. *poketto* (pocket)

5. *setto* (set)   10. *roketto* (rocket)

*From Dutch, *kok*

F. Read the following words and write them in Romanized Japanese.

1. エチケット (etiquette)   5. バスケットボール (basketball)

2. クラリネット (clarinet)   6. ピクニック (picnic)

3. サンドイッチ (sandwich)   7. ホットドッグ (hot dog)

4. デラックス (deluxe)   8. スリッパ (slipper)

Component Words

Another symbol seen in Katakana writing is the solid dot placed in the middle of the line • to show the components of an expression. This dot separates words in a compound expression consisting of three or more words, for example, エス・オー・エス (SOS). It is sometimes used in two-word expressions for clarity, as in アブストラクト・アート (abstract art). It is also used when one or more of the words is a proper noun, for example:

ケネディー・ライブラリー   ヤンキー・スタジアム

(Kennedy Library)   (Yankee Stadium)

There is no spelling rule that specifies the solid dot as the only symbol used for this purpose. There have been other proposals for a suitable symbol, such as:

アメリカン ＝フットボール　　アメリカンーフットボール

(American football)

Among these possibilities, the separation of words by a solid dot is the most prevalent, so it is used in this workbook. Some other examples are:

ステップ・バイ・ステップ　(step by step)

ギブ・アンド・テーク　(give and take)

ケース・バイ・ケース　　(case by case)

シンクロナイズド・スイミング　(synchronized swimming)

Other Modifications

Yōon

There are two groups of yōon in Katakana writing. The first group of thirty-three contracted syllables duplicates those found in the Hiragana syllabary. The second group of twenty-five syllables was created to expand the range of options in writing loanwords and other foreign words in Katakana.

Making the first group of yōon in Katakana is done exactly the same way as in Hiragana. All the symbols that represent a consonant + the vowel [i] become contracted syllables when combined with a small [ya], [yu] or [yo]. All of the first group of contracted syllables are presented in the basic Katakana syllabary (section 3 of table I on p. 12). Remember that yōon are written with a full-size Katakana plus a half-size [ya], [yu] or [yo]. The following is a summary of which syllables are formed in which way.

1. For example: KI (キ) + YA (ヤ) = KYA (キャ), as in the *kya* of *kyandē* (candy).

The syllables that belong to this group, besides [ki] and [gi], are [ni], [hi], [bi], [pi], [mi] and [ri], and, of course, all combine with [yu] and [yo] as well as [ya].

2. For example: CHI (チ) + YA (ヤ) = CHA (チャ), as in the *cha* of *chansu* (chance).

The other syllables formed in this way are [chu], [cho], [sha], [shu], and [sho].

3. For example: JI (ジ) + YU (ユ) = JU (ジュ), as in the [ju] of *jūsu* (juice). Also, [ja] as in *jazu* (jazz) and [jo] as in *Jon* (John) are formed in this way.

Exercises

G. Fill in each space with the proper contracted syllable to form a word.

1. ___ ンプ° (camp)
   kya

2. ___ ロット (culotte)
   kyu

3. ___ ウリュウ (dinosaur)
   kyo

4. ___ ツ (shirt)
   sha

5. リフレッ ___ メント (refresh-
   shu   ment)

6. レセプ° ___ ン (reception)
   sho

7. ___ ンピオン (champion)
   cha

9. ___ ウ (butterfly)
   cho

10. コ ___ ック (cognac)
    nya

11. ___ ーズ (news)
    nyu

12. ___ キ ___ キ (one after
    nyo *nyo*   another)

13. ___ ーズ (fuse)
    hyu

14. ___ ウ (leopard)
    hyo

15. ___ ージカル (musical)
    myu

8. アマ ___ ア (amateur)
   _{chu}

16. ___ ウ (dragon)
    _{ryu}

H. Write the following words in Katakana, paying special attention to the contracted syllable.

1. *kyabetsu* (cabbage)

2. *kyūri* (cucumber)

3. *gyōza** (a small dumpling)

4. *jamu* (jam)

5. *junia* (junior)

6. *jōkā* (joker)

7. *kechappu* (ketchup)

8. *suchuwādesu* (stewardess)

9. *chokorēto* (chocolate)

10. *Nyūton* (Newton)

11. *intabyū* (interview)

12. *hyōtan* (bottle gourd)

13. *komyunisuto* (communist)

14. *ryūmachi*** (rheumatism)

*From Chinese, *chiao tzu*   **From Dutch, *rheumatisch*

I. Read the following words and write them in Romanized Japanese.

1. グランドキャニオン (Grand Canyon)

2. マニキュア (manicure)

3. シャンペン (champagne)
   シャンパン

4. チャレンジ (challenge)

8. コンピュータ (ー) (computer)

9. ヒューヒュー (with a whistle)

10. ヒョロヒョロ (staggering)

11. ミュンヘン ＊ (Munich)

34

5. チューインガム (chewing gum) 12. リュックサック ** (rucksack)

6. イチョウ (ginkgo tree) 13. ギャラリー (gallery)

7. メニュー (menu) 14. ジュピター (Jupiter)

*From German, München **From German, *Rucksack*

The Expanded Syllabary

As noted previously, besides the basic yōon, there are twenty-five more syllables that have been created expressly to write foreign words. All but one of these (*vu*) are yōon. These additional syllables are a device used to suggest the closest pronunciation of the foreign word.

There is a difference of opinion within the Kokugo Shingikai (Japanese Language Council) concerning how certain words should be written. For example, there is the question of whether to write ヴェイオリン or the simpler バイオリン for "violin"; フィルム or the simpler フイルム for "film," and so on. In this workbook, both variations are given because one provides the closest link to the original pronunciation and allows the student to see the correlation between the Japanese and the source word, while the other version may be just as common and equally acceptable.

Exercises

J. Fill in each space with the proper contracted syllable to form a word.

1. ___ ― ト (quart)
   kwo

12. ___ ― ク (fork)
    fo

2. ___ フ (chef)
   she

13. ___ イオリン (violin)
    va

3. エー＿＿ント (agent)
_je_

14. ＿＿クトリア (Victoria)
_vi_

4. パー＿＿ー (party)
_ti_

15. ランデ＿＿ー (rendezvous)
_vu_

5. ＿＿オール (Dior)
_di_

16. ＿＿ール (veil)
_ve_

6. プロ＿＿ーサー (producer)
_du_

17. ＿＿リューム (volume)
_vo_

7. ＿＿ス (chess)
che

18. ＿＿ルソン (Wilson)
_wi_

8. フィレン＿＿* (Florence)
tse

19. ＿＿ートレス (waitress)
_we_

9. ＿＿ン (fan)
_fa_

20. ＿＿ッチ (watch)
_wo_

10. ＿＿ルム (film)
_fi_

21. ＿＿ーター (water)
_wo_

11. ＿＿ンシング (fencing)
_fe_

*From Italian, Firenze

K. Write the following words in Katakana, paying special attention to the underlined contracted syllable.

1. _jetto_ (jet)

5. _chero_ (cello)

9. _fōmaru_ (formal)

2. _tī_ (tea)

6. _famirī_ (family)

10. _Vachikan_ (Vatican)

3. *biru*d*ingu* (building)   7. *o*f*isu* (office)   11. *Wīn** (Vienna)

4. *du*etto (duet)   8. *f*eminisuto (feminist)   12. *wōtāsukī* (water ski)

*From German, Wien

L. Read the following words and write them in Romanized Japanese.

1. シェーカー   (shaker)

2. プロジェクト   (project)

3. ディズニーランド   (Disney-land)

4. チェック   (check)

5. ファッション   (fashion)

6. フィクション   (fiction)

7. ニューフェース   (new face)

8. シンフォニー   (symphony)

9. ヴァージニア   (Virginia)
   バージニア

10. ヴェニス   (Venice)
   ベニス

11. ヴォルガ   (Volga)
   ボルガ

12. ヴィスコンシン   (Wisconsin)

13. ヴェブスター   (Webster)

14. ヴォーカー   (walker)

3

WORDS OF JAPANESE ORIGIN

Students of Japanese may be aware that Katakana is used for writing onomatopoeic expressions, but they may not know the many other uses of this syllabary. Conventional uses range from domestic telegrams to the names of plants and animals. Then there is the recent trend for words in Katakana to be used in newspapers, magazines and advertisements instead of Kanji or Hiragana. There are many reasons for this. One is that many Kanji have dropped out of daily use, or it may just be simpler to write the intended meaning in Katakana due to the complexity of the Kanji. Another reason is that Katakana adds emphasis to words that would appear ordinary if written in Hiragana.

Currently there are no explicit standards for using Katakana for emphasis, and in many cases usage may depend on how an author chooses to express himself.

The following exercises present a variety of words that are always or sometimes written in Katakana. They have been arranged in a number of categories to better give the idea of the variety of uses.

Names of Plants and Animals

The common names of plants and animals may be written in either Hiragana or Katakana. Guidelines generally suggest that Katakana be used.

Of course, the long ō is treated as two separate syllables and written with the vowel ウ , or sometimes オ , but not with the long-vowel mark ー or ｜ .

Exercises

A. Write the following names of plants in Katakana.

1. *momo* (peach)

2. *kashi* (oak)

3. *matsu* (pine)

4. *sakura* (cherry blossom)

5. *bara* (rose)

6. *himawari* (sunflower)

7. *ninjin* (carrot)

8. *tamanegi* (onion)

B. Write the following names of animals in Katakana.

1. *kaeru* (frog)

2. *saru* (monkey)

3. *uma* (horse)

4. *hatsukanezumi* (mouse)

5. *suzume* (sparrow)

6. *karasu* (crow)

7. *hibari* (lark)

8. *kakkō* (cuckoo)

9. *tsubame* (swallow)

10. *tsuru* (crane)

11. *fuka* (shark)

12. *maguro* (tuna)

13. *tako* (octopus)

14. *buri* (yellowtail)

15. *awabi* (abalone)

C. Read the following names of plants and write them in Romanized Japanese.

1. ハ ヽ ス (lotus)

2. ク ス (camphor tree)

7. タ ケ (bamboo)

8. ナ ン テ ン (nandina)

39

3. ソテツ (sago palm)

4. ウメ (apricot)

5. スイセン (narcissus)

6. モミジ (maple)

9. スミレ (violet)

10. リンゴ (apple)

11. シイタケ (mushroom)

12. ワカメ (*wakame* seaweed)

D. Read the following names of animals and write them in Romanized Japanese.

1. クマ (bear)

2. ニワトリ (chicken)

3. キリン (giraffe)

4. カモ (wild duck)

5. キリギリス (grasshopper)

6. カモシカ (serow)

7. ホタル (firefly)

8. ワニ (crocodile)

9. ミツバチ (honeybee)

10. インコ (parakeet)

11. ガン (wild goose)

12. ハマグリ (clam)

13. ニシン (herring)

14. イワシ (sardine)

15. クジラ (whale)

16. ヒラメ (flatfish)

17. カメ (turtle)

18. マス (trout)

Onomatopoeia

By onomatopoeia we mean a term that expresses its own definition by imitating the sound associated with it or by naming such a sound. Examples include the characteristic sounds of animals or birds, inanimate sounds of nature—such as wind, rain and flowing water—and all kinds of other sounds heard in daily life. Other words describe movement or the state of things graphically or suggestively. Expressions of this sort are known as mimesis, and they are more commonly, though not exclusively, written in Hiragana. Onomatopoeia does, of course, exist in English as well, e.g. *bow-wow, cuckoo, pitter-patter* and so on. However, in Japanese, these types of expression occur with much greater frequency, to the point that the foreign student of the language is sometimes nearly overwhelmed. At the same time such study reveals one of the more fascinating aspects of the language.

In the following exercises, remember that a long vowel when it occurs is expressed by either — or | .

Exercises

E. The following are sounds made by animals. Write the onomatopoeic words in Katakana.

1. *wanwan* (bow-wow)

2. *nyānyā* (meow-meow)

3. *kokekokkō* (cock-a-doodle-do)

4. *chūchū* (squeak-squeak)

5. *mōmō* (moo-moo)

6. *konkon* (yelp of fox)

7. *būbū* (oink-oink)

8. *gāgā* (quack-quack)

9. *kākā* (caw-caw)

10. *hōhokekyo* (cry of bush warbler)

F. The following are other sounds, some made by inanimate objects. Write the onomatopoeic words in Katakana.

1. *potopoto* (dripping)

2. *zāzā* (pouring rain)

3. *shitoshito* (drizzling rain)

4. *sarasara* (gurgling [stream])

5. *byūbyū* (whistling [wind])

6. *gorogoro* (thundering)

7. *karakoro* (clop-clop of *geta*)

8. *pishan* (slapping)

9. *patan* (slamming)

10. *tonton* (rapping)

G. The following refer to movement or condition. Write the mimetic words in Katakana.

1. *kirakira* (glittering)

2. *pikapika* (shiny)

3. *dokidoki* (throbbing)

4. *harahara* (thrilling)

5. *kutakuta* (worn to a frazzle)

6. *pechapecha* (chattering)

7. *meramera* (burst into flames)

8. *ukiuki* (cheerful)

9. *punpun* (strong smelling)

10. *hirahira* (fluttering)

H. Read the following onomatopoeic and mimetic words and write them in Romanized Japanese.

1. ピョピョ (peep-peep) 15. チリンチリン (ting-a-ling)

42

2. リーンリーン　(chirping of bush cricket)

3. ピーチクパーチク　(sound of lark)

4. ガヤガヤ　(buzzing voices)

5. キャンキャン　(yelping [dog])

6. ジージー　(chirping cicada)

7. チンチロリン　(chirping cricket)

8. ヒーン　(neighing)

9. ガタガタ　(rattling)

10. カチン　(clinking)

11. ガリガリ　(scratching)

12. ピューピュー　(whistling [wind])

13. ゴツン　(bumping [head])

14. ドンドン　(banging [drum])

16. ゲラゲラ　(cackle)

17. ワイワイ　(clamoring voices)

18. ザブザブ　(splashing)

19. チクチク　(prickly)

20. ツルツル　(slippery)

21. ツンツン　(haughty)

22. バラバラ　(scattered)

23. ボロボロ　(crumbling)

24. バタバタ　(flapping)

25. ブツブツ　(muttering)

26. チカチカ　(smarting eyes)

27. ギラギラ　(dazzling)

28. ソワソワ　(restless)

Domestic Telegrams

A long-established use of Katakana is in domestic telegrams. Study the following examples.

「アシタ イク ムカエ タノム」
Ashita   iku   mukae   tanomu   (Coming tomorrow. Please meet [me].)

「カネ オクレ」
Kane   okure   (Send money.)

「ニュウガク オメデトウ」
Nyūgaku   omedetō   (Congratulations on getting into the school [of your choice].)

As shown here, particles and punctuation are generally omitted and the plain forms of verbs are used rather than the more polite *-masu/desu* forms.

New Uses

In this section we will take note of words as they appear in newspapers, magazines and advertisements when they are written in Katakana, either to replace disused or complicated Kanji or to give them uniqueness or emphasis.

The following are examples taken from current magazines and newspapers. As noted previously, there is little standardization in this application of Katakana. Why Katakana is used as it is here may be difficult to understand at this point. For the time being, it is enough to simply read the words in question. When a more advanced level is reached, they can be studied again along with additional examples.

To Replace *Kanji*

1. カエル は どんな エサ を たべますか。

Kaeru wa donna esa o tabemasu ka. (What kind of food do frogs eat?)

44

2. むこうの ヤブ の なか に イヌ がいる。

   Mukō no yabu no naka ni inu ga iru. (There is a dog in the grove over there.)

3. ハマキ を すった。

   Hamaki o sutta. ([I] smoked a cigar.)

4. よく きょうだいゲンカ を する。

   Yoku kyōdaigenka o suru. (Those brothers and sisters often fight among themselves.)

5. カギ を おとした。

   Kagi o otoshita. ([I] dropped the key.)

6. メガネ が みえない。

   Megane ga mienai. ([I] can't find my glasses.)

7. イトコ がきた。

   Itoko ga kita. ([My] cousin came.)

8. フンイキ があかるい。

   Fun'iki ga akarui. (It has a friendly atmosphere.)

9. ツエ を ついて あるく。

   Tsue o tsuite aruku. ([I] walk with a cane.)

10. あし が マヒ した。

    Ashi ga mahi shita. ([My] leg became paralyzed.)

For Emphasis

In the following examples, the underlined words are written in Katakana for emphasis. Note that some of the sentences contain idioms or idiomatic expressions, so a literal translation would be misleading. The English sentences give the meaning as a whole, and some of the underlined words are glossed with their usual meaning.

1. 「行っては ダメ」と クギ をさした。

   "Itte wa dame," to kugi o sashita. ([I] warned him not to go. [*Dame*, "no good"; *kugi*, "nail."])

2. ツケ が まわって きた。

   Tsuke ga mawatte kita. ([I] must pay for my sins. [*Tsuke*, "bill."])

3. チリ も つもれば 山 と なる。

   Chiri mo tsumoreba yama to naru. (If particles of dust are piled up, they can grow into a mountain.)

4. そんな こと は カンタン ですよ。

   Sonna koto wa kantan desu yo. (Such a thing is simple.)

5. そと は マックラ だ。

   Soto wa makkura da. (It is pitch-black outside.)

6. バカサワギ を している。

   Bakasawagi o shite iru. ([They're] acting wild.)

7. フツウ の コップ を つかう。

   Futsū no koppu o tsukau. ([I] use an ordinary cup.)

8. キモノ すがた。

   Kimono sugata. (Dressed in a kimono.)

9. あの 人 は カンジ がいい。

   Ano hito wa kanji ga ii. (That person makes a favorable impression.)

10. まいばん <u>ハシゴ</u>ざけをする。

Maiban <u>hashigo</u>zake o suru. ([He] goes barhopping every night. [*Hashigo*, "ladder."])

11. <u>フタ</u>をあけてみる。

<u>Futa</u> o akete miru. ([I can] see the final results. [*Futa*, "lid."])

12. あそこの<u>ダシ</u>と<u>タレ</u>は おいしい。

Asoko no <u>dashi</u> to <u>tare</u> wa oishii. (Their soup <u>stock</u> and [savory] <u>sauce</u> are good.)

13. かれは <u>シロ</u>か<u>クロ</u>か。

Kare wa <u>shiro</u> ka <u>kuro</u> ka. (Is he <u>innocent</u> or <u>guilty</u>?)

14. <u>マジメ</u>な かんきゃくは <u>イイカゲン</u>だとおこる。

<u>Majime</u> na kankyaku wa <u>iikagen</u> da to okoru. (A <u>serious</u> audience gets angry if it is an <u>unconvincing</u> performance.)

15. <u>ワイロ</u>をうけとる。

<u>Wairo</u> o uketoru. ([He] accepts <u>bribes</u>.)

16. <u>ヤマ</u>をむかえた。

<u>Yama</u> o mukaeta. ([It] has reached the <u>peak</u>.)

Other Uses

In addition to the foregoing examples, there are a few others, both conventional and newly created. For example, in the classic Nō play, such terms as シテ (leading role), ワキ (supporting role), and ツレ (companion role) are written in Katakana.

Another example of conventional usage is the writing of Kanji pronunciation, in dictionaries, for example, but in other places, too. The *kun* (Japanese) reading is normally given in Hiragana, while the *on* (Chinese) reading is generally in Katakana.

Until the early 1980s, Katakana only was the common form of writing for all computer work. The latest advances in hard- and software have offered the possibility of inputting and printing Hiragana and even Kanji, but Katakana continues to play the major role, probably because of its simplicity and legibility. Another place it is frequently found is on the many forms we are forever filling out, along with or in place of other writing.

Another new trend is for companies to propagate their corporate, brand and/or trade names in Katakana, for example, トヨタ (the auto maker), セイコー (watches) and キッコーマン (soy sauce).

Terms for furniture, utensils or tools are occasionally seen in Katakana, e.g., タンス (chest of drawers), ナベ (pan), カマ (rice cooker), カンナ (carpenter's plane) and オノ (axe).

Sometimes colloquial expressions are written in Katakana: ノッポ (tall person), チビ (short person), デブ (fat person), and so on.

Finally, an exclamation or a tag question may be in Katakana, although the rest of the sentence is in Hiragana. This is probably done for emphasis. Note the following examples.

あつい ナア‥　　　(Oh, how hot it is!)

アーア、‥‥　　　(Oh, my!)

‥‥だよ ネ.　　　(. . . isn't it?)

4

WORDS OF FOREIGN ORIGIN

As experts have pointed out and students will sooner or later discover, Japanese has a rich and varied vocabulary. We indicated on page 9 that imported words are generally categorized as being from Chinese (and associated with Kanji), or as coming from other—generally Western—languages. If the latter have been assimilated, they are called *gairaigo* (loanwords). The earliest borrowings of this sort were from Portuguese in the 16th century and, a few decades later, from the Dutch.

Currently, the greatest number of new words come into Japanese from English, which surely occupies first place as a source language for loanwords, as well as of the constant flow of temporary vocabulary that does not become assimilated. Another sizable category of words written in Katakana includes proper nouns such as geographic and personal names. Here, transcription often follows the spelling/pronunciation pattern of the original language.

The number of items in all categories is quite large; in fact, there are a number of gairaigo dictionaries. One reason for these borrowings is that it is simpler to make use of words, especially scientific and technical terms, as they are by transcribing them into Katakana than it is to find or create suitable Kanji. Also, the freshness of foreign words written in either Katakana or the Roman alphabet appeals to the Japanese penchant for borrowing ideas. Examples are notably conspicuous in the many foreign words seen in shop names, brand names, designers' names, recipes and commercials. Moreover, it is structurally easy to use such imports in a Japanese sentence. *Suru* added after words makes verbs, e.g., drive + *suru*, ドライヴする. Adding *na* after words makes them function as adjectives, e.g., smooth + *na*, スムー

ズな. Words followed by *ni* are like adverbs of a certain type, e.g., smooth + *ni*, スムーズに.

Guidelines for Transcription

Reading and writing gairaigo and other foreign words involves close attention and care in the study of Katakana. Moreover, pronunciation should be taken into consideration whenever possible.

This chapter examines the methods for transcribing foreign words based on the guidelines established by the Ministry of Education, the Textbook Research Center and the Japanese Language Council. There are slight differences in the way the three bodies have chosen to transcribe certain words, and alternatives have been pointed out in the guidelines. As you will see, the system is logical and functional, even though consistency does not reach 100 percent.

On page 11, we noted that the reason for the expanded Katakana syllabary was to indicate pronunciation not found in Japanese (table II, p. 13). On the one hand, quite a number of words can be transcribed more or less directly into their Japanese pronunciation, e.g., *kī* (key). At other times, there are sounds or combinations of sounds that have no exact counterpart in Japanese, so a certain amount of adaptation is necessary, often depending for its effectiveness on the expanded syllabary.

It may happen that a speaker of English, for example, will come across a borrowed word and not recognize either the origin or the original pronunciation. This can be rather confusing if the source word and the English word are similar, e.g., *ryūmachi*, rheumatism, from Dutch, *rheumatisch*. Fortunately, the number of such cases is not so great, but it is a point worth remembering.

The following compilation of patterns does not cover every situation. However, they are valuable for establishing a firm but flexible foundation. Using them, a student should be able to learn quickly how to read and write words of foreign origin.

1. English words having the voiceless *th* sound: this *th* is replaced by サ *sa*, シ *shi*, ス *su*, セ *se* or ソ *so*, as in the following examples.

third	サード	three	スリー
thinner	シンナー	birthday	バースデー
Smith	スミス	theory	セオリー
bath towel	バスタオル	authority	オーソリティー

テーマ (*tēma*, theme) seems to be an exception, but actually it is based on the German *Thema*.

2. English words having *f* + vowel and not transcribed by フ *fu*: these become ファ *fa*, フィ *fi*, フェ *fe*, フォ *fo* but are sometimes represented by the more traditional ハ *ha*, ヒ *hi*, ヘ *he*, ホ *ho*. Note that some words are correctly written using either alternative.

fantasy	ファンタジー	coffee	コーヒー
film	フィルム	uniform	ユニフォーム ユニホーム
fence	フェンス	platform	プラットフォーム プラットホーム
formal	フォーマル	microphone	マイクロフォン マイクロホン

3. Similarly, English *v* + vowel become ヴァ *va*, ヴィ *vi*, ヴ *vu*, ヴェ *ve*, ヴォ *vo*, but sometimes are represented by the more traditional バ *ba*, ビ *bi*, ブ *bu*, ベ *be*, ボ *bo*. Note that some words almost always appear using the latter syllables, while others are acceptable in either form.

violin	ヴァイオリン バイオリン	casting vote	キャスティング・ヴォート キャスティング・ボート
victory	ヴィクトリー ビクトリー	overcoat	オーバー
rendezvous	ランデヴー ランデブー	vitamin	ビタミン
veil	ヴェール ベール	curve	カーブ
vocabulary	ヴォキャブラリー ボキャブラリー	elevator	エレベーター

In words like those in the following examples, the underlined syllables are written with the traditional syllables ヒュ *hyu* and ビュ *byu*.

<u>fu</u>se	ヒューズ	<u>view</u>point	ビューポイント
re<u>view</u>	レビュー	re<u>vue</u>	レビュー

4. In transcribing the English sounds represented by *t* + vowel as in *tea* and *tick*, ティ *ti* is used in some cases, as indicated in the examples below on the left, and in other cases the more traditional チ *chi* is commonly used, as in the words on the right.

variety	ヴァラエティー バラエティー	ticket	ティケット チケット
teacher	ティーチャー	tip	チップ
T-shirt	ティーシャツ	team	ティーム チーム

Similarly, ディ *di* is replaced in certain cases by the customarily used ジ *ji*. Note the following examples.

building   ビルディング   radio   ラジオ

dinner   ディナー   dilemma   ジレンマ

dictation   ディクテーション   Edison   エジソン

accordion   アコーディオン   Scandinavia   スカンジナヴィア

5. In words like the examples, *t* + vowel becomes チュ [chu] in all cases.

stewardess スチュワーデス   tube チューブ   tulip チューリップ

Similarly, when the English is *d* + vowel as in *due*, the Katakana is デュ *dyu* or, in some cases, the more traditional ジュ *ju*.

Dupont   デュポン   producer   プロデューサー

duplicator   デュプリケーター   schedule   スケジュール

6. In the case of words like those listed below, the English [t] sound is replaced by the syllable ト [to], but occasionally by ツ [tsu].

gentleman   ジェントルマン   (Christmas) tree   クリスマス・ツリー

hot　ホット　　　　　　　　　two-piece　ツーピース

cut　カット

In the same manner, the English [d] sound is replaced by the syllable ド [do]. The following are some examples.

handbag　ハンドバッグ　　drama　ドラマ　　drive　ドライヴ

7. The syllable ア [a] is used to transcribe *a* when the letter *a* happens to follow the letter *i*, as in the examples on the left below. When the *a* is pronounced like the vowel in *nut* or is silent, words are customarily written with ヤ [ya], as in the three examples on the right.

piano　ピアノ　　　　　　　diamond　ダイヤモンド

Niagara　ナイアガラ　　　　diagram　ダイヤグラム

Miami　マイアミ　　　　　　dial　ダイヤル

In writing gairaigo (just as in spelling English) logical explanations for the way certain words are written are by no means self-evident, so the words should simply be memorized when they are first encountered.

8. For English *sh* + vowel as in *shake* or *shed* the syllable セ *se* is sometimes used instead of シェ *she*. The following are some examples of both ways.

shade　シェード　　　　　　shepherd　シェパード
　　　　　　　　　　　　　　　　　　　セパード

54

sherry　シェリー　　　　　　　　milk shake　ミルク セーキ

In the same manner, for English *je* or *ge*,　ジェ　*je* may be replaced by　ゼ *ze* as seen in the words on the right.

jet　ジェット　　　　　　　　　Argentina　アルゼンチン

Nigeria　ナイジェリア　　　　　　angel　エンゼル

9. According to the guidelines laid down by the Japanese Language Council and the Textbook Research Center, in ordinary words (excepting those transcribed by the basic *wa*) English *w/wh* + vowel is transcribed by the two syllable [u] + [i]　ウイ　, [u] + [e]　ウエ　or [u] + [o]　ウオ . However, when the word is a proper noun, *w/wh* + vowel is represented by the contracted syllables　ヴィ　[wi],　ヴェ　[we] or　ヴォ　[wo] instead of the vowel combinations.

Proper nouns　　　　　　　　　Words

Wilson　　ヴィルソン　　　　　whiskey　ウイスキー

Wilcox　　ヴィルコックス　　　wave　　ウエーブ

Midway　　ミッドヴェー　　　　wedding　ウエディング

Kuwait　　クヴェート　　　　　watch　　ウオッチ

Milwaukee　ミルヴォーキー　　　water　　ウオーター

This rule can be bent if the contracted syllables seem closer to the original word. Thus　ウイスキー　and　ウオッチ　may become　ヴィスキー　and

55

ウォッチ if the writer believes that this creates a more accurate sound.

10. The English *qu* in words such as *Quaker* is generally written with the two symbols [ku] + [e]: クエ . An exception is seen in words using the contracted syllable クォ [kwo], like クォーター (quarter), クォータ (quota), etc.

square スクエア Quaker クエーカー

Similarly, the *gua* in words like Guam, Paraguay and Guatemala is represented by the two symbols [gu] + [a] グア.

Paraguay パラグアイ Guatemala グアテマラ Guam グアム

11. Usually, for English words ending in *ium*, or sometimes just *um*, the transcription is ウム *umu*. However, ニューム *nyūmu* is also seen in some dictionaries and other places. Study the following examples.

aluminum アルミニウム
          アルミニューム   radium ラジウム

A few such words end with *amu* as in スタジアム (stadium).

12. When English *r* comes after a vowel in the same syllable, the transcription is usually done by representing the vowel sound and lengthening it with — or ｜ . Examples of this include the following.

car カー   skirt スカート

scarf スカーフ   curb カーブ

mixer ミキサー   course コース

letter レター   color カラー

maker	メーカー	sports	スポーツ
lighter	ライター	corn	コーン
girl	ガール	professor	プロフェッサー

There are also words transcribed without — or 丨, such as:

career	キャリア	chair	チェア	gear	ギア

In a few cases, this "r" is kept by using the syllable ル [ru]. ビール (beer) and ベルモット (vermouth) are examples of this, as are メートル (meter) and some other metric units.

13. In most cases the English syllable *-ture* is transcribed by — or 丨 after チャ *cha*. Examples are:

lecture	レクチャー	picture	ピクチャー
culture	カルチャー	nature	ネーチャー
adventure	アドベンチャー	mixture	ミックスチャー

Another way of representing this syllable is チュア *chua*, as in the following examples.

caricature	カリカチュア	mature	マチュア

14. English words spelled with two consecutive vowel letters are often transcribed with — or 丨. Note that there are a number of different vowels in the examples below, and that the point here is only the vowel length in transcription. The original vowel sounds may be long or short. Study the ex-

amples carefully.

chain	チェーン	speed	スピード	boom	ブーム
sauce	ソース	beef	ビーフ	moon	ムーン
automatic	オートマチック	chief	チーフ	boot	ブーツ
beach	ビーチ	soap	ソープ	group	グループ
pearl	パール	coach	コーチ	fruit	フルーツ
speech	スピーチ	wool	ウール	suit	スーツ

In some words, generally when the syllable ends with *d*, *k*, *p*, or *ch*, — or ｜ is not used but a half-sized ツ [tsu] is inserted. Examples of this are:

bread	ブレッド	look	ルック
head	ヘッド	goodbye	グッドバイ
cook	コック	touch	タッチ
book	ブック	couple	カップル

There are some words that do not fall into either category. Such words must simply be learned one by one. The following are examples.

| door | ドア | bearing | ベアリング | fair | フェア |

15. When there is a silent *e* at the end of a word or syllable and the vowel letter is not *i*, — or ｜ often comes after the vowel in that syllable.

skate	スケート	lane	レーン	pole	ポール
case	ケース	rebate	リベート	flute	フルート
cane	ケーン	tape	テープ°	ice cube	アイスキューブ
sale	セール	hope	ホープ°	crepe	クレープ°

16. Usually, words ending with a *w* or *y* have the vowel lengthened with — or] . The following are examples.

show	ショー	window	ウィンドー	copy	コピ°ー
stew	シチュー	ability	アビリティー	honey	ハニー

17. As seen in the following examples, the vowel-lengthening — or] comes in the middle of words where the syllable *-tion* is immediately preceded by a vowel, except when the vowel letter is *i*.

inflation	インフレーション	motion	モーション
intonation	イントネーション	lotion	ローション
sensation	センセーション	carnation	カーネーション
frustration	フラストレーション	decoration	デコレーション

18. The symbol indicating a double consonant, the half-sized ツ [tsu], is also inserted in a word when the English spelling is *ck*, *x*, *tch* and *dge*. These spellings typically occur at the end of syllables.

luck	ラック	telex	テレックス	judge	ジャッジ

rock	ロック	box	ボックス	badge	バッジ
deck	デッキ	switch	スイッチ		
lock	ロック	catch	キャッチ		

Loanwords

There are many sources of loanwords in Japanese. Some date so far back that native speakers who are not specialists may be unaware of their foreign origin. These words from Portuguese are examples: カルタ *karuta* (*carta*, card), カッパ *kappa* (*cappa*, raincoat), ビロード *birōdo* (*veludo*, velvet), カステラ *kasutera* (*castella*, sponge cake) and many more. Certain other assimilated words are still recognized as being of foreign origin: オーバー *ōbā* (overcoat), ハンカチ *hankachi* (handkerchief), ラジオ *rajio* (radio), and so on. Then there are a lot more words taken directly from English in more recent times and given a Japanese pronunciation, for example ディスカッション *disukasshon* (discussion), ジェネレーション *jenerēshon* (generation), etc.

There are among these words some that have been shortened. *Ōbā* is one such word, as are パソコン *pasokon* (personal computer), デモ *demo* (demonstration), マスコミ *masukomi* (mass communication) and so on. The tendency to abbreviate is somewhat more conspicuous now than formerly.

Unabbreviated Words

The following exercises will give practice in reading and writing foreign words in Katakana.

Exercises

Write the following words in Katakana, applying the guidelines studied previously. (The number in parentheses indicates the number of syllables.)

A. Words starting with [a] ∼ [o] or [we], [wo].

1. iron (4)

2. alphabet (6)

3. idea (4)

4. asphalt (5)

5. ink (3)

6. information (7)

7. instant (6)

8. image (4)

9. wood (3)

10. wink (4)

11. whiskey (5)

12. wedding (4)

13. Walkman (5)

14. engine (4)

15. escalator (7)

16. expert (6)

17. orange (4)

18. Olympic (6)

19. olive (4)

20. oatmeal (6)

B. Words starting with [ka] ∼ [ko], etc.

1. calcium (5)

2. cover (3)

3. gasoline (4)

4. key (2)

11. gate (3)

12. comedy (4)

13. concert (5)

14. golf (3)

5. king (3)

6. gift (3)

7. cleaning (6)

8. club (3)

9. gray (3)

10. cable car (6)

15. cabin (3)

16. cabinet (5)

17. gap (3)

18. gamble (4)

19. cue (2)

20. quality (4)

C. Words starting with [sa] ∼ [so], etc.

1. service (4)

2. salad (3)

3. seat (3)

4. scene (3)

5. jeans (4)

6. steak (4)

7. stereo (4)

8. zoom lens (6)

9. center (4)

10. sense (3)

11. zero (2)

12. soda (3)

13. shampoo (4)

14. jazz (2)

15. shoes (3)

16. juice (3)

17. show (2)

18. joke (3)

19. shepherd (4)

20. generation (6)

D. Words starting with [ta] ～ [to], etc.

1. taxi (4)
2. typewriter (7)
3. dance (3)
4. diamond (6)
5. tip (3)
6. two-piece (5)
7. text (4)
8. technique (5)
9. dessert (4)
10. decoration (6)

11. top (3)
12. dressing (6)
13. channel (4)
14. tulip (5)
15. chalk (3)
16. teapot (5)
17. disk (3)
18. display (5)
19. duty (4)
20. cherry (3)

E. Words starting with [na] ～ [no], etc.

1. nylon (4)
2. napkin (4)
3. needle (4)
4. nuance (4)

5. nude (3)
6. negative (4)
7. normal (4)
8. novel (4)

F. Words starting with [ha] ～ [ho], etc.

1. hamburger (6)

2. hiking (5)

3. banana (3)

4. pilot (5)

5. puzzle (3)

6. heater (4)

7. business (4)

8. pilaf (3)

9. pizza (2)

10. flight (4)

11. free (3)

12. brand (4)

13. blond (4)

14. present (5)

15. plastic (6)

16. helper (4)

17. bed (3)

18. belt (3)

19. page (3)

20. pen (2)

21. hotel (3)

22. bonus (4)

23. poster (4)

24. human (4)

25. beautiful (5)

26. fight (3)

27. finance (5)

28. field (4)

29. ferry (3)

30. focus (4)

G. Words starting with [ma] ～ [mo], [ya] ～ [yo], etc.

1. mask (3)

2. market (5)

3. mat (3)

4. magic (4)

5. mint (3)

6. mystery (5)

7. mink (3)

8. mood (3)

9. melon (3)

10. memory (4)

11. medal (3)

12. motorboat (7)

13. model (3)

14. Yankee (4)

15. unit (4)

16. unique (4)

17. yolk (3)

18. musician (5)

H. Words starting with [ra] ～ [ro] or [wa].

1. line (3)

2. rival (4)

3. life (3)

4. license (5)

5. risk (3)

6. recital (5)

10. rule (3)

11. rate (3)

12. reception (5)

13. level (3)

14. raincoat (6)

15. robot (4)

7. ring (3)

8. leader (4)

9. ruby (3)

16. romantic (6)

17. wine (3)

18. wax (4)

I. Words starting with [va] ～ [vo] ([ba], [bi], [be], [bo]).

1. vanilla (3)

2. vitality (6)

3. violet (6)

4. variation (6)

5. video (3)

6. viola (3)

7. veteran (4)

8. velvet (5)

9. volt (3)

10. vogue (3)

In exercises J through R, read the Katakana and write the original English word. If a word is not from English, as indicated by the asterisk, simply read the word and write it as Romanized Japanese.

J. Words starting with [a] ～ [o], [wi], [we] or [wo].

1. アクセサリー

2. アナウンサー

3. アドレス

4. アカデミー

5. アルバイト *

8. インテリア

9. インスピレーション

10. ウラン *

11. エキゾチック

12. エレガント

15. オルガン

16. オーケストラ

17. オリジナル

18. ヴィッチ

19. ウィット

6. イヤリング　　13. エレクトロニクス　20. ウェイジ

7. イデオロギー *　14. エピソード　　21. ウォールストリート

K. Words starting with [ka] ～ [ko], etc.

1. カセット　　　8. クーポン　　　15. コミュニケーション

2. カーディガン　9. クラシック　　16. ゴム *

3. カレンダー　　10. グレープジュース　17. ゴシップ

4. カクテル　　　11. ケンブリッジ　18. キャッシュ

5. ガイド　　　　12. ゲスト　　　19. ギャランティー

6. キッチン　　　13. コンタクト・レンズ　20. キューピー

7. ギター　　　　14. コンサルタント　21. クォーテーション・
　　　　　　　　　　　　　　　　　　　　マーク

L. Words starting with [sa] ～ [so], etc.

1. サイクリング　　8. ズーム　　　　15. ジャーナリスト

2. サンタクロース　9. セールスマン　16. シュークリーム *

3. シンプル　　　10. セーター　　　17. ショーウインドー

4. ジングルベル　11. ゼロックス　　18. ショック

5. スナック　　　12. ソファー　　　19. ジョギング

6. ストレス　　　13. シャワー　　　20. シェープ

67

7. スモッグ゛ 14. ジャケット 21. ジェネレーター

M. Words starting with [ta] ～ [to], etc.

1. タバコ 8. デート 15. ドライヤー

2. タレント 9. デモクラシー 16. チャーター

3. ダイヴィング゛
   ダイビング゛ 10. デザイナー 17. チャンネル

4. チキンライス 11. トーナメント 18. チェックアウト

5. チアリーダー 12. トピック 19. ティーンエージャー

6. ツーリスト 13. トランジスタ(ー) 20. ディレクター

7. テント 14. ドーナッツ 21. デュプレックス

N. Words starting with [na] ～ [no], etc.

1. ナイター 5. ヌガー * 9. ノスタルジア

2. ナレーション 6. ネックレス 10. ノイローゼ *

3. ニコチン * 7. ネーブル 11. ニュークリア

4. ニーソックス 8. ネームバリュー 12. ニュートラル

O. Words starting with [ha] ～ [ho], etc.

1. ハイヒール 9. プライベート 17. ヒューマニズム

2. バーベキュー 10. ヘリコプター 18. ビューティーサロン

3. パスポート   11. ベストセラー   19. ピューリタン

4. ヒーロー   12. ペイデー   20. ファイナル

5. ビニール   13. ホームシック   21. フィアンセ

6. ピーナッツ   14. ボタン   22. フェアプレー

7. フットボール   15. ボイコット   23. フェスティバル

8. ブラウス   16. ポピュラー   24. フォーチュン

P. Words starting with [ma] ～ [mo], [ya] ～ [yo], etc.

1. マネージャー   7. メディア   13. ヤング・レディー

2. マーガリン   8. メッセージ   14. ユーモア

3. マッサージ   9. メロディー   15. ユートピア

4. ミシン   10. モノレール   16. ヨーグルト

5. ミサイル   11. モットー   17. ヨット

6. ムーヴィー   12. モニター   18. ミュージアム
　ムービー

Q. Words starting with [ra] ～ [ro] or [wa]

1. ラブレター   7. ルーレット   13. ロビー

2. ラッシュアワー   8. ルームメート   14. ワイシャツ
　　　　　　　　　　ルームメイト

3. ラグビー   9. ルート   15. ワルツ

4. リハーサル   10. レストラン *   16. ワンピース

5. リーグ   11. レタス

6. リムジン   12. ロースト・ビーフ

R. Words starting with [va] ～ [vo] ([ba], [bi], [be], [bo]).

1. ヴァンパイヤー / バンパイヤー
2. ヴィザ / ビザ
3. ヴィジョン / ビジョン
4. ヴィーナス / ビーナス
5. ヴェニヤ / ベニヤ
6. ヴェスト / ベスト
7. ヴォキャブラリー / ボキャブラリー
8. ヴォーカリスト / ボーカリスト

Abbreviated Words

Because of the abbreviation in this type of word, it may be difficult to recognize the original word. Study the following examples carefully.

1. アニメ   (animation)
2. イラスト   (illustration)
3. インテリ   (intelligentsia)
4. インフレ   (inflation)
5. エンスト   (engine stall)*
6. エレキ   (electric guitar)
16. デパート   (department store)
17. ハンスト   (hunger strike)
18. ハイテク   (high technology)
19. パトカー   (patrol car)
20. パソコン   (personal computer)
21. パート   (part-timer)

70

7. エアコン　(<u>air con</u>ditioner)　　22. ビル　(<u>buil</u>ding)

8. ギャラ　(<u>guara</u>ntee)　　23. ベア　(<u>base up</u>)**

9. コネ　(<u>con</u>nection)　　24. マスコミ　(<u>mass communication</u>)

10. スーパー　(<u>super</u>market)　　25. マザコン　(<u>mother complex</u>)

11. スト　(<u>st</u>rike)　　26. マンネリ　(<u>manneri</u>sm)

12. セコハン　(<u>seco</u>nd<u>hand</u>)　　27. ミニコン　(<u>minicom</u>puter)

13. テレビ　(<u>televi</u>sion)　　28. ラジカセ　(<u>radio-casse</u>tte tape recorder)

14. デモ　(<u>demo</u>nstration)　　29. リモコン　(<u>remo</u>te <u>con</u>trol)

15. デフレ　(<u>defl</u>ation)　　30. ワープロ　(<u>word</u> <u>pro</u>cessor)

*lit., engine stop

**From *bēsuappu*, a made-in-Japan expression meaning a raise in the basic wage.

Sometimes a word is formed by combining an abbreviated foreign word with a Japanese word, for example, カラオケ : *kara* (empty) + *oke* (*ōkesutorēshon*, orchestration). This is a stereo system with taped accompaniment, mike and mixer for sing-along.

Proper Nouns

Geographic Names

Read the Katakana for the following sample of geographic names. Identify

71

the words in English, keeping in mind that some are derived from languages other than English.

アジア Asia

1. アフガニスタン
2. イスラエル
3. イラン
4. インド
5. カンボジア
6. サウジアラビア

7. ソヴィエト
   ソビエト
8. タイ
9. ニューデリー
10. ネパール
11. バンコク
12. ヒマラヤ

13. フィリピン
14. ヴェトナム
    ベトナム
15. ホンコン
16. マニラ
17. マレーシア
18. レバノン

アフリカ Africa

1. アルジェリア
2. エジプト

3. キリマンジャロ
4. ケープタウン

5. サハラ
6. ナイル

オーストラリア／ニュージーランド Australia/New Zealand

1. ウェリントン
2. シドニー
3. メルボルン

サウス・アメリカ South America

1. アマゾン
2. アルゼンチン

5. エクアドル
6. コロンビア

9. ブラジル
10. ペルー

3. アンデス   7. チリ   11. リオデジャネイロ

4. ヴェネズエラ 8. ブエノスアイレス 12. リマ
   ベネズエラ

ノース・アメリカ North America

1. アラスカ   6. ニューヨーク   11. ボストン

2. エルサルバドル 7. ハワイ   12. マッキンリー

3. カナダ   8. パナマ   13. メキシコ

4. キューバ   9. ヴァンクーヴァー 14. ロスアンゼルス
          バンクーバー   ロサンゼルス

5. サンフランシスコ 10. フロリダ   15. ワシントン

ヨーロッパ Europe

1. アテネ   8. スウェーデン   15. ベルギー

2. アルプス   9. セーヌ   16. ポーランド

3. イギリス   10. デンマーク   17. マドリード

4. オーストリア   11. ドイツ   18. モスクア

5. ギリシア   12. ノルウェー   19. ユーゴスラヴィア
               ユーゴスラビア

6. グリーンランド 13. パリ   20. ローマ

7. スイス   14. フランス   21. ロンドン

Personal Names

The following list presents in random order surnames and given names, names that are famous and names that are not. Study them carefully and see how many you can identify.

1. ダーウィン

2. トム

3. レオナルド・ダ・ヴィンチ
　レオナルド・ダビンチ

4. ジョイス

5. ヘップバーン

6. スターリン

7. ナンシー

8. ソクラテス

9. ツルゲーネフ

10. リチャード

11. エドワード

12. パスカル

13. ナポレオン

14. バッハ

24. エリザベス

25. メンデルスゾーン

26. アイゼンハワー

27. レーニン

28. ブラウン

29. モーツァルト

30. キャレン

31. コロンブス

32. ジュリー

33. ロックフェラー

34. ジョン

35. ケネディ（ー）

36. マッカーサー

37. マルクス

15. メリー

16. リンカーン

17. フィリップ

18. チャイコフスキー

19. イングリッド・バーグマン

20. バイロン

21. ピカソ

22. ミケランジェロ

23. シェークスピア

38. チャップリン

39. ミッチェル

40. セザンヌ

41. マリリン・モンロー

42. キャサリン

43. ハイドン

44. カント

45. ピーター

46. アインシュタイン

5

REVIEW EXERCISES

On the following pages are exercises designed to give practice in using the Katakana you have now mastered.

Part A of the exercises shows symbols that must be clearly distinguished so as not to make mistakes when reading and writing Katakana. The two exercises B and C deal with the recognition of Katakana. Part D is an exercise in recognizing correct usage. Exercise E emphasizes the writing of Katakana in sentences. Do these exercises as rapidly as possible.

A. Common Mistakes

1. Katakana that look alike or that are often confused with each other.

2. Katakana that look like Hiragana.

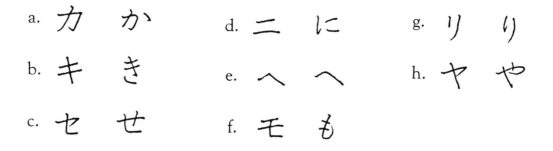

B. Recognition Exercise

Find the Katakana symbol that matches each Romanized syllable written to the left of the vertical line. Try to go as fast as you can, avoiding mistakes.

o	テ	イ	ケ	ホ	チ	オ	ネ
nu	ス	ネ	ヌ	メ	ン	フ	ノ
i	レ	メ	イ	ノ	ソ	ト	オ
su	タ	ス	フ	ム	マ	ア	ヌ
a	マ	タ	ヤ	ア	ワ	ケ	ナ
ka	か	ケ	ヘ	カ	ク	ラ	サ
yu	ヨ	ユ	モ	コ	ロ	ミ	ヒ
ma	ウ	ム	ナ	ス	ヤ	マ	ユ
re	ル	ワ	し	ヘ	レ	リ	ト
n	ン	ノ	シ	ツ	ハ	ナ	ソ
gya	ぎゃ	ギュ	キャ	キュ	ギャ	キョ	ギョ
ho	ハ	ヨ	モ	ホ	ヒ	オ	セ
bu	プ	ビ	ブ	ヴ	フ	バ	ベ
ri	ル	り	エ	リ	レ	ノ	ト
ki	ミ	ニ	き	モ	チ	キ	テ
wa	ワ	ウ	ク	ケ	ナ	ラ	カ
pyo	ヒョ	ピュ	ピャ	ビョ	ピョ	ビャ	ビュ
se	サ	セ	ス	エ	セ	ヤ	ソ
ge	グ	げ	ケ	ダ	ゲ	ガ	デ
u	ワ	ケ	ウ	ク	フ	ラ	ア
e	キ	ヨ	エ	コ	ニ	ヒ	ユ
jo	ジュ	ギョ	シュ	ジョ	ショ	ジャ	シャ
chi	キ	モ	ナ	テ	サ	チ	フ

C. Hidden Word Puzzle

At the bottom of the page are thirty-two words written in Roman letters. Try to find them in the Katakana maze. The words may be written from left to right, top to bottom or diagonally (left to right only). No words are written backwards. Circle them as you find them. There may be other hidden words besides those listed. See how many you can find.

ウ	カ	メ	ラ	コ	ー	ル	ヴィ	ネ	キョ	テ	フ	ヨ	ー	ロ	ッ	パ	ノ
ペ	タ	ト	レ	ス	ト	ラ	ン	マ	ア	ニ	タ	ア	オ	ツ	イ	シ	キ
エ	シャ	カ	セ	ハ	ン	チョ	ニ	ア	イ	ス	ク	リ	ー	ム	マ	ノ	ミ
ケ	ン	サ	ナ	ファ	ン	ヘ	ト	ソ	・	サ	リ	ヒョ	ネ	ム	レ	ヤ	ハ
ー	ペ	シ	エ	ノ	ダ	カ	ル	ワ	ミャ	ー	ス	ケ	ヒャ	ア	ン	ツ	ソ
ア	ン	マ	レ	ロ	マ	ン	チ	ッ	ク	オ	マ	レ	ニ	ネ	ベ	ス	ワ
コ	ヌ	ロ	ベ	パ	モ	バ	エ	ピ	プ	ネ	ス	タ	レ	キャ	ツ	ル	シ
プ	ヒュ	ヨ	ー	チャ	ヴ	ス	テ	ミョ	サ	ク	ゴ	チュ	マ	ン	ヴァ	キ	ン
ロ	ー	ジョ	タ	イ	ジ	ケ	ク	チ	ッ	タ	ミ	ニ	ビ	デ	イ	ジュ	ト
グ	デュ	イ	ー	ニュ	ス	ッ	ショ	ソ	ズ	イ	ハ	レ	シュ	ー	オ	チョ	ン
ラ	ノ	ス	リョ	ワ	ピ	ト	ノ	ー	ト	ン	テ	キュ	フ	リャ	リ	コ	マ
ム	ヴォ	ア	ウ	ン	リュ	ボ	ニャ	ミ	ル	ク	ソ	イ	マ	サ	ン	レ	ディ
フェ	ジ	ニョ	リ	ワ	ム	ー	コ	ー	ヒ	ー	ナ	ビャ	チ	ピョ	オ	ー	ヌ
ア	チェ	オ	ス	ン	フィ	ル	ム	テ	マ	ッ	チ	ヤ	ワ	イ	ン	ト	ヴォ
ソ	ッ	ケ	ジェ	ゾ	ペ	ネ	オ	ン	・	サ	イ	ン	フォ	ム	リ	ス	ト
ミャ	ー	ミャ	ー	ティ	ー	ヴィ	リ	ヴェ	コ	ン	ピュ	ー	タ	ー	ビュ	ソ	ジャ

aisukurīmu	Orimpikku	kyandē	terebi	basukettobōru	myāmyā	Washinton
Ajia	kamera	shampen	naifu	matchi	Yōroppa	wanwan
inku	Kurisumasu	sokkusu	neon sain	puroguramu	risuto	
erebētā	kompyūtā	chokorēto	nekutai	firumu	resutoran	
omuretsu	kyabetsu	tenisu	hankachi	miruku	romanchikku	

78

D. Usage Exercise

In the following *a* & *b* pairs, choose the correct one on the basis of the guidelines you have learned.

1. a. ニューヨーク
   b. ニュウヨウク

2. a. ダイヤモンド
   b. ダイアモンド

3. a. チョー
   b. チョウ

4. a. ポケット
   b. ポッケト

5. a. ベイスボール
   b. ベースボール

6. a. ピ゜ヤノ
   b. ピ゜アノ

7. a. ラジオ
   b. ラディオ

8. a. アルゼンチン
   b. アルジェンチン

9. a. ステュワーデス
   b. スチュワーデス

10. a. グァム
    b. グアム

11. a. サンドイッチ
    b. サンドウイッチ

12. a. ウィルソン
    b. ウイルソン

13. a. ドアー
    b. ドア

14. a. ニャアニャア
    b. ニャーニャー

15. a. コーヒー
    b. コーフィー

16. a. パーチー
    b. パーティー

17. a. プロデューサー
    b. プロジューサー

18. a. クリスマス・トリー
    b. クリスマス・ツリー

19. a. ミルクシェーキ
    b. ミルクセーキ

20. a. ジェット
    b. ゼット

E. Writing Sentences

Write the following sentences in Japanese in the space provided. Pay particular attention to which words should be written in Hiragana and which in Katakana.

1. Sumisu-san wa Rosuanzerusu no kompyūta no kaisha de hataraite imasu.

   (Mr. Smith works at a computer company in Los Angeles.)

2. Depāto de burausu to sētā to sukāto o kaimashita. (I bought a blouse, a sweater and a skirt at the department store.)

3. Jon to Merī wa resutoran de wain to sarada to sutēki o tanomimashita. (John and Mary ordered wine, salad and steak at the restaurant.)

4. Tēburu no ue ni wa fōku to naifu to supūn ga arimashita. Kirei na napukin to koppu mo arimashita. (There were forks, knives and spoons on the table. There were also pretty napkins and cups.)

5. Dezāto ni aisukurīmu to appuru pai o tabemashita. (They had ice cream and apple pie for dessert.)

6. Kinō wa ame ga zāzā futta node, uchi de terebi o mimashita. (Because it rained hard yesterday, I stayed home and watched TV.)

7. Kōen ni wa kirei na bara to tsutsuji ga takusan saite imashita. (Many beautiful roses and azaleas were blooming in the park.)

8. Naiagara no taki wa Kanada kara mo Amerika kara mo miemasu. (Niagara Falls can be seen from both Canada and the United States.)

9. Jōji to Kyasarin wa Yōroppa ni ikimashita. Pari de atarashii fasshon o takusan mimashita. (George and Katherine went to Europe. In Paris they saw many new fashions.)

10. Wiruson-san wa itsumo uīkuendo ni haikingu ni ikimasu. Tokidoki basukettobōru mo shimasu. (Mr. Wilson always goes hiking on weekends. He sometimes plays basketball, too.)

11. Sutereo de yoku kurashikku no rekōdo o kikimasu. (I often listen to classical records on [my] stereo.)

12. Tonari no pātī de otona wa bīru ya uisukī o nonde imasu ga, kodomo wa jūsu ya kokakōra o nonde imasu. (At the party next door, the adults are drinking beer and whiskey, but the children are drinking juice and Cocacola.)

13. "Ranchi ni hambāgā o tabemasu ka, hottodoggu o tabemasu ka."
"Iie, watashi wa karēraisu o tabemasu." ("Are you going to have a hamburger or a hot dog for lunch?" . . . "No, I'm having curried rice.")

14. Kare wa komedī ga suki desu ga, watashi wa romanchikku na eiga ga suki desu. (He likes comedies, but I like romantic movies.)

15. Ano shoppingu sentā no naka ni bēkarī ga arimasu. Soko no chīzukēki to shūkurīmu wa totemo oishii desu. (There's a bakery in that shopping center. Their cheesecake and cream puffs are very good.)

APPENDIX A: Exercise Answers

Chapter 4

Exercise A

1. アイロン 2. アルファベット 3. アイディア 4. アスファルト 5. インク 6. インフォメーション 7. インスタント 8. イメージ 9. ウッド 10. ウインク 11. ウイスキー 12. ウェディング 13. ウォークマン 14. エンジン 15. エスカレーター 16. エキスパート 17. オレンジ 18. オリンピック 19. オリーブ 20. オートミール

Exercise B

1. カルシウム 2. カバー 3. ガソリン 4. キー 5. キング 6. ギフト 7. クリーニング 8. クラブ 9. グレー 10. ケーブルカー 11. ゲート 12. コメディー 13. コンサート 14. ゴルフ 15. キャビン 16. キャビネット 17. ギャップ 18. ギャンブル 19. キュー 20. クォリティー

Exercise C

1. サービス 2. サラダ 3. シート 4. シーン 5. ジーンズ 6. ステーキ 7. ステレオ 8. ズームレンズ 9. センター 10. センス 11. ゼロ 12. ソーダ 13. シャンプー 14. ジャズ 15. シューズ 16. ジュース 17. ショー 18. ジョーク 19. シェパード 20. ジェネレーション

Exercise D

1. タクシー 2. タイプライター 3. ダンス 4. ダイヤモンド 5. チップ 6. ツーピース 7. テキスト 8. テクニック 9. デザート 10. デコレーション 11. トップ 12. ドレッシング 13. チャンネル 14. チューリップ 15. チョーク 16. ティーポット 17. ディスク 18. ディスプレー 19. デューティー 20. チェリー

Exercise E

1. ナイロン 2. ナプキン 3. ニードル 4. ニュアンス 5. ヌード 6. ネガティブ 7. ノーマル 8. ノベル/ノヴェル

Exercise F

1. ハンバーガー 2. ハイキング 3. バナナ 4. パイロット 5. パズル 6. ヒーター
7. ビジネス 8. ピラフ 9. ピザ 10. フライト 11. フリー 12. ブランド 13. ブロンド 14. プレゼント 15. プラスチック 16. ヘルパー 17. ベッド 18. ベルト
19. ページ 20. ペン 21. ホテル 22. ボーナス 23. ポスター 24. ヒューマン
25. ビューティフル 26. ファイト 27. ファイナンス 28. フィールド 29. フェリー
30. フォーカス

Exercise G

1. マスク 2. マーケット 3. マット 4. マジック 5. ミント 6. ミステリー 7. ミンク 8. ムード 9. メロン 10. メモリー 11. メダル 12. モーターボート 13. モデル 14. ヤンキー 15. ユニット 16. ユニーク 17. ヨーク 18. ミュージシャン

Exercise H

1. ライン 2. ライバル 3. ライフ 4. ライセンス 5. リスク 6. リサイタル 7. リング 8. リーダー 9. ルビー 10. ルール 11. レート 12. レセプション 13. レベル 14. レインコート 15. ロボット 16. ロマンチック 17. ワイン 18. ワックス

Exercise I

1. ヴァニラ/バニラ 2. ヴァイタリティー/バイタリティー 3. ヴァイオレット/バイオレット 4. ヴァリエーション/バリエーション 5. ヴィデオ/ビデオ 6. ヴィオラ/ビオラ 7. ヴェテラン/ベテラン 8. ヴェルベット/ベルベット 9. ヴォルト/ボルト
10. ヴォーグ/ボーグ

Exercise J

1. accessory 2. announcer 3. address 4. academy 5. *arubaito* (from German, *Arbeit*) part-time or temporary job 6. earring 7. *ideorogī* (from German, *Ideologie*) ideology 8. interior 9. inspiration 10. *uran* (from German, *Uran*) uranium 11. exotic 12. elegant 13. electronics 14. episode 15. organ 16. orchestra 17. original 18. witch 19. wit 20. wage 21. Wall Street

Exercise K

1. cassette 2. cardigan 3. calendar 4. cocktail 5. guide 6. kitchen 7. guitar 8. coupon 9. classic 10. grape juice 11. Cambridge 12. guest 13. contact lens 14. consultant 15. communication 16. *gomu* (from Dutch, *gom*) rubber 17. gossip 18. cash 19. guarantee 20. Kewpie 21. quotation mark

Exercise L

1. cycling   2. Santa Claus   3. simple   4. jingle bells   5. snack   6. stress   7. smog   8. zoom   9. salesman   10. sweater   11. Xerox   12. sofa   13. shower   14. jacket   15. journalist   16. *shūkurīmu* (from French, *chou à la crème*) cream puff   17. show window   18. shock   19. jogging   20. shape   21. generator

Exercise M

1. tobacco   2. talent   3. diving   4. chicken rice   5. cheerleader   6. tourist   7. tent   8. date   9. democracy   10. designer   11. tournament   12. topic   13. transistor   14. doughnut   15. dryer   16. charter   17. channel   18. check out   19. teenager   20. director   21. duplex

Exercise N

1. nighter (night game)   2. narration   3. nicotine (from German, *Nikotin*)   4. knee sock   5. *nugā* (from French, *nougat*) nougat   6. necklace   7. navel   8. name value   9. nostalgia   10. *noirōze* (from German, *Neurose*) neurosis   11. nuclear   12. neutral

Exercise O

1. high heels   2. barbecue   3. passport   4. hero   5. vinyl   6. peanut   7. football   8. blouse   9. private   10. helicopter   11. best seller   12. payday   13. homesick   14. button   15. boycott   16. popular   17. humanism   18. beauty salon   19. Puritan   20. final   21. fiance   22. fair play   23. festival   24. fortune

Exercise P

1. manager   2. margarine   3. massage   4. (sewing) machine   5. missile   6. movie   7. media   8. message   9. melody   10. monorail   11. motto   12. monitor   13. young lady   14. humor   15. Utopia   16. yogurt   17. yacht   18. museum

Exercise Q

1. love letter   2. rush hour   3. rugby   4. rehearsal   5. league   6. limousine   7. roulette   8. roommate   9. route   10. restaurant (from French, *restaurant*)   11. lettuce   12. roast beef   13. lobby   14. (dress) shirt   15. waltz   16. one-piece

Exercise R

1. vampire   2. visa   3. vision   4. Venus   5. veneer   6. vest   7. vocabulary   8. vocalist

Geographic Names

Asia: 1. Afghanistan 2. Israel 3. Iran 4. India 5. Kampuchea (Cambodia) 6. Saudi Arabia 7. Soviet (Union) 8. Thailand 9. New Delhi 10. Nepal 11. Bangkok 12. Himalayas 13. (The) Philippines 14. Vietnam 15. Hong Kong 16. Manila 17. Malaysia 18. Lebanon

Africa: 1. Algeria 2. Egypt 3. Kilimanjaro 4. Cape Town 5. Sahara 6. Nile

Australia/New Zealand: 1. Wellington 2. Sydney 3. Melbourne

South America: 1. Amazon 2. Argentina 3. (The) Andes 4. Venezuela 5. Ecuador 6. Columbia 7. Chile 8. Buenos Aires 9. Brazil 10. Peru 11. Rio de Janeiro 12. Lima

North America: 1. Alaska 2. El Salvador 3. Canada 4. Cuba 5. San Francisco 6. New York 7. Hawaii 8. Panama 9. Vancouver 10. Florida 11. Boston 12. (Mt.) McKinley 13. Mexico 14. Los Angeles 15. Washington

Europe: 1. Athens 2. Alps 3. England 4. Austria 5. Greece 6. Greenland 7. Switzerland 8. Sweden 9. Seine 10. Denmark 11. Germany 12. Norway 13. Paris 14. France 15. Belgium 16. Poland 17. Madrid 18. Moscow 19. Yugoslavia 20. Rome 21. London

Personal Names

1. Darwin 2. Tom 3. Leonardo da Vinci 4. Joyce 5. Hepburn 6. Stalin 7. Nancy 8. Socrates 9. Turgenev 10. Richard 11. Edward 12. Pascal 13. Napoleon 14. Bach 15. Mary 16. Lincoln 17. Phillip 18. Tchaikovsky 19. Ingrid Bergman 20. Byron 21. Picasso 22. Michelangelo 23. Shakespeare 24. Elizabeth 25. Mendelssohn 26. Eisenhower 27. Lenin 28. Brown 29. Mozart 30. Karen 31. Columbus 32. Julie 33. Rockefeller 34. John 35. Kennedy 36. MacArthur 37. Marx 38. Chaplin 39. Mitchell 40. Cezanne 41. Marilyn Monroe 42. Katherine 43. Haydn 44. Kant 45. Peter 46. Einstein

Chapter 5

Exercise D

1. a 2. a 3. b 4. a 5. b 6. b 7. a 8. a 9. b 10. b 11. a 12. a 13. b 14. b 15. a 16. b 17. a 18. b 19. b 20. a

Exercise E

1. スミスさんは　ロスアンゼルスの　コンピューターの　かいしゃで　はたらいています。

2. デパートで　ブラウスと　セーターと　スカートを　かいました。

3. ジョンと　メリーは　レストランで　ワインと　サラダと　ステーキを　たのみました。

4. テーブルの　うえには　フォークと　ナイフと　スプーンが　ありました。きれいな　ナプキンと　コップも　ありました。

5. デザートに　アイスクリームと　アップルパイを　たべました。

6. きのうは　あめが　ザーザー　ふったので、うちで　テレビを　みました。

7. こうえんには　きれいな　バラと　ツツジが　たくさん　さいていました。

8. ナイアガラのたきは　カナダからも　アメリカからも　みえます。

9. ジョージと　キャサリンは　ヨーロッパに　いきました。パリで　あたらしいファッションを　たくさん　みました。

10. ウィルソンさんは　いつも　ウイークエンドに　ハイキングに　いきます。ときどき　バスケットボールも　します。

11. ステレオで　よく　クラシックの　レコードを　ききます。

12. となりの　パーティーで　おとなは　ビールや　ウイスキーを　のんでいますが、こどもは　ジュースや　コカコーラを　のんでいます。

13. 「ランチに　ハンバーガーを　たべますか、ホットドッグを　たべますか。」
「いいえ、わたしは　カレーライスを　たべます。」

14. かれは　コメディーが　すきですが、わたしは　ロマンチックな　えいがが　すきです。

15. あの　ショッピング・センターの　なかに　ベーカリーが　あります。そこの　チーズケーキと　シュークリームは　とても　おいしいです。

APPENDIX B: The Derivation of Katakana

The Hiragana syllabary was used at the time of its invention in the 9th century primarily by women. As a rule, only men wrote in Kanji. Prime users were monks who copied Buddhist scripture and other writings. They had to indicate the pronunciation of often very complicated Chinese characters, and they needed a mnemonic device of fairly simple form. It was for this purpose that Katakana was created, at about the same time as Hiragana. Both syllabaries were standardized by the Ministry of Education in the late 19th century.

Rather than reproduce the whole character in a cursive style, the method adopted for Katakana was to select a particular element in one of several ways.

1. Complete borrowing of simple strokes:

千 → チ   二 → ニ   八 → ハ

2. Taking the left side (first) strokes:

加 → カ *   伊 → イ   祢 → ネ

3. Taking the top (first) strokes:

宇 → ウ   牟 → ム

4. Taking the right side (last) strokes:

江 → エ   奴 → 又   礼 → レ

The forty-six basic Katakana are listed on the next page in their usual order, in vertical rows beginning at the upper right. This is the same as the Katakana Syllabary on page 12. To the right of each symbol is the Kanji from which it was derived.

*Note that Hiragana and Katakana [ka] are derived from the same Kanji, as are [ne], [u], [nu], [re] and a number of others.

ナ奈	タ多	サ散	カ加	ア阿
ニ二	チ千	シ之	キ幾	イ伊
ヌ奴	ツ川	ス須	ク久	ウ宇
ネ祢	テ天	セ世	ケ介	エ江
ノ乃	ト止	ソ曽	コ己	オ於

ワ和	ラ良	ヤ也	マ末	ハ八
	リ利		ミ三	ヒ比
	ル流	ユ由	ム牟	フ不
	レ礼		メ女	ヘ部
ヲ乎	ロ呂	ヨ与	モ毛	ホ保

ン尓	

カタカナ   Let's Learn Katakana

1985 年10月　第 1 刷発行
2010 年 6 月　第23刷発行

著　者　ヤスコ・コサカ・ミタムラ
発行者　廣田浩二
発行所　講談社インターナショナル株式会社
　　　　〒112-8652 東京都文京区音羽 1-17-14
　　　　電話　03-3944-6493（編集部）
　　　　　　　03-3944-6492（マーケティング部・業務部）
　　　　ホームページ　www.kodansha-intl.com

印刷・製本所　大日本印刷株式会社

落丁本・乱丁本は購入書店名を明記のうえ、小社業務部宛にお送りください。送料小社負担にてお取替えします。なお、この本についてのお問い合わせは、編集部宛にお願いいたします。本書の無断複写（コピー）、転載は著作権法の例外を除き、禁じられています。

定価はカバーに表示してあります。

© ヤスコ・コサカ・ミタムラ 1985
Printed in Japan
ISBN 978-4-7700-1219-7